Vacation Mandala
Escape Coloring

Adult Relaxation

Sans Sargent

www.glendowermedia.com

Copyright 2016
Glendower Media

More Coloring Fun
For The Whole Family

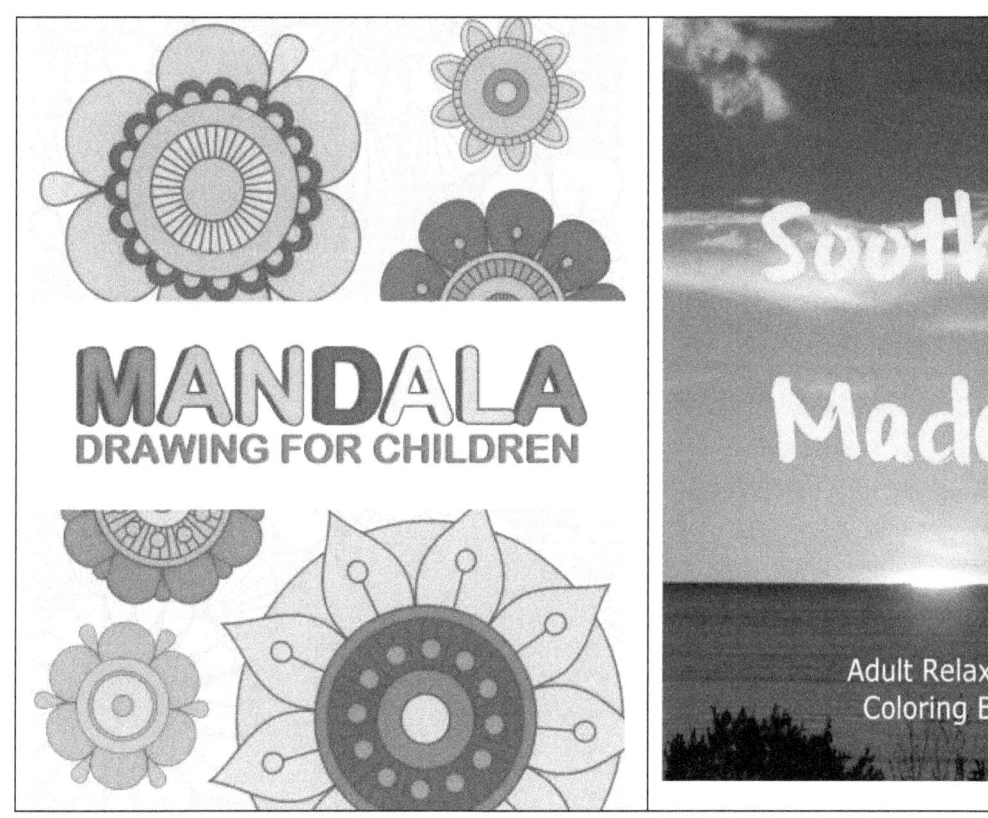 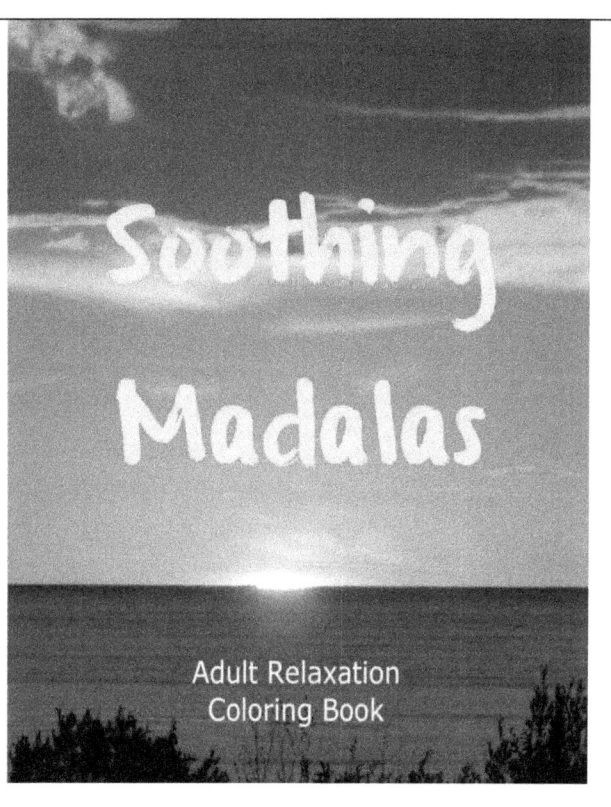

Fine coloring and puzzle books for the family at our website www.glendowermedia.com.

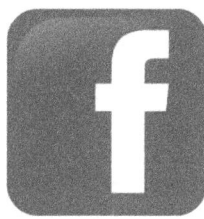

Like us on

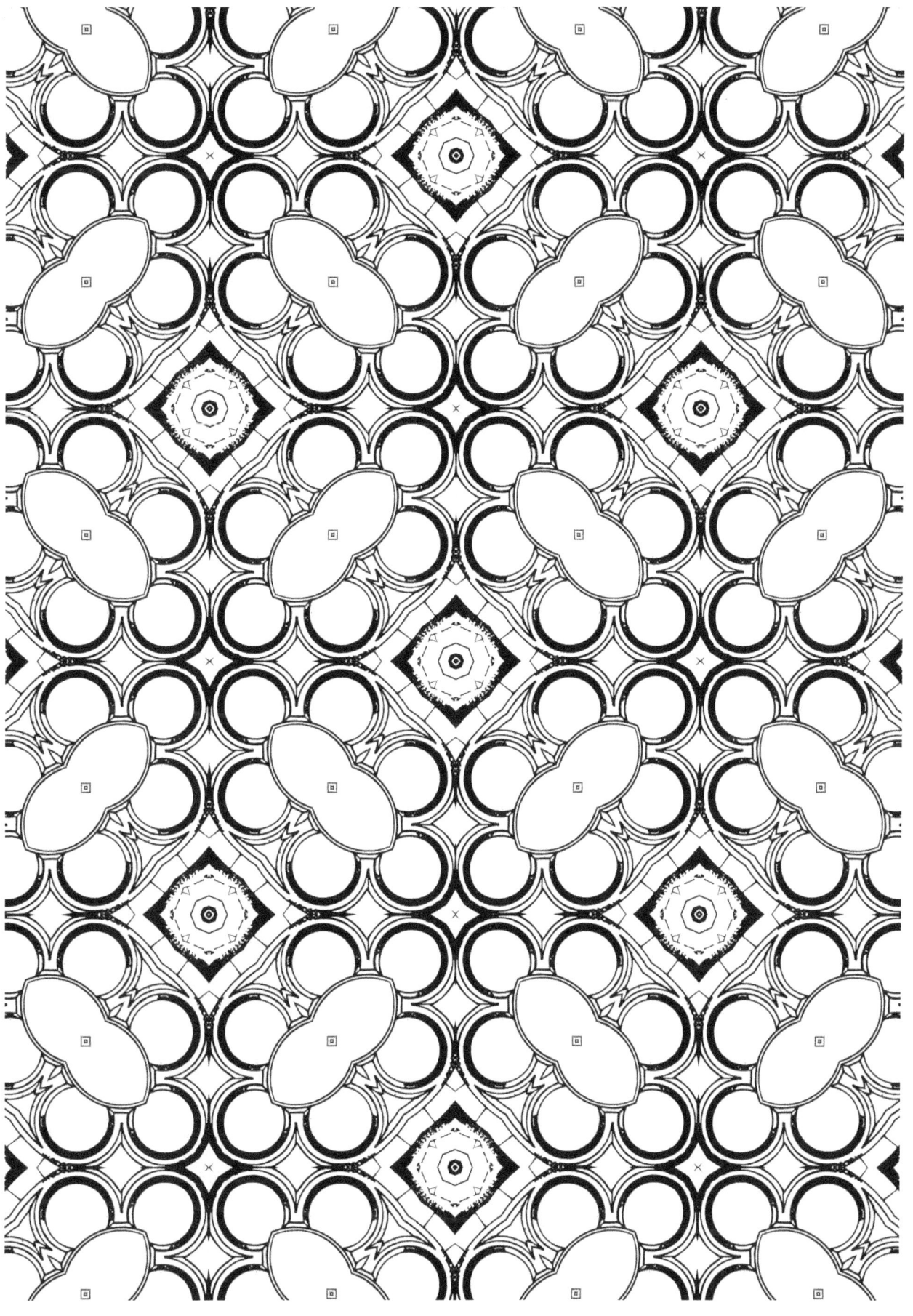

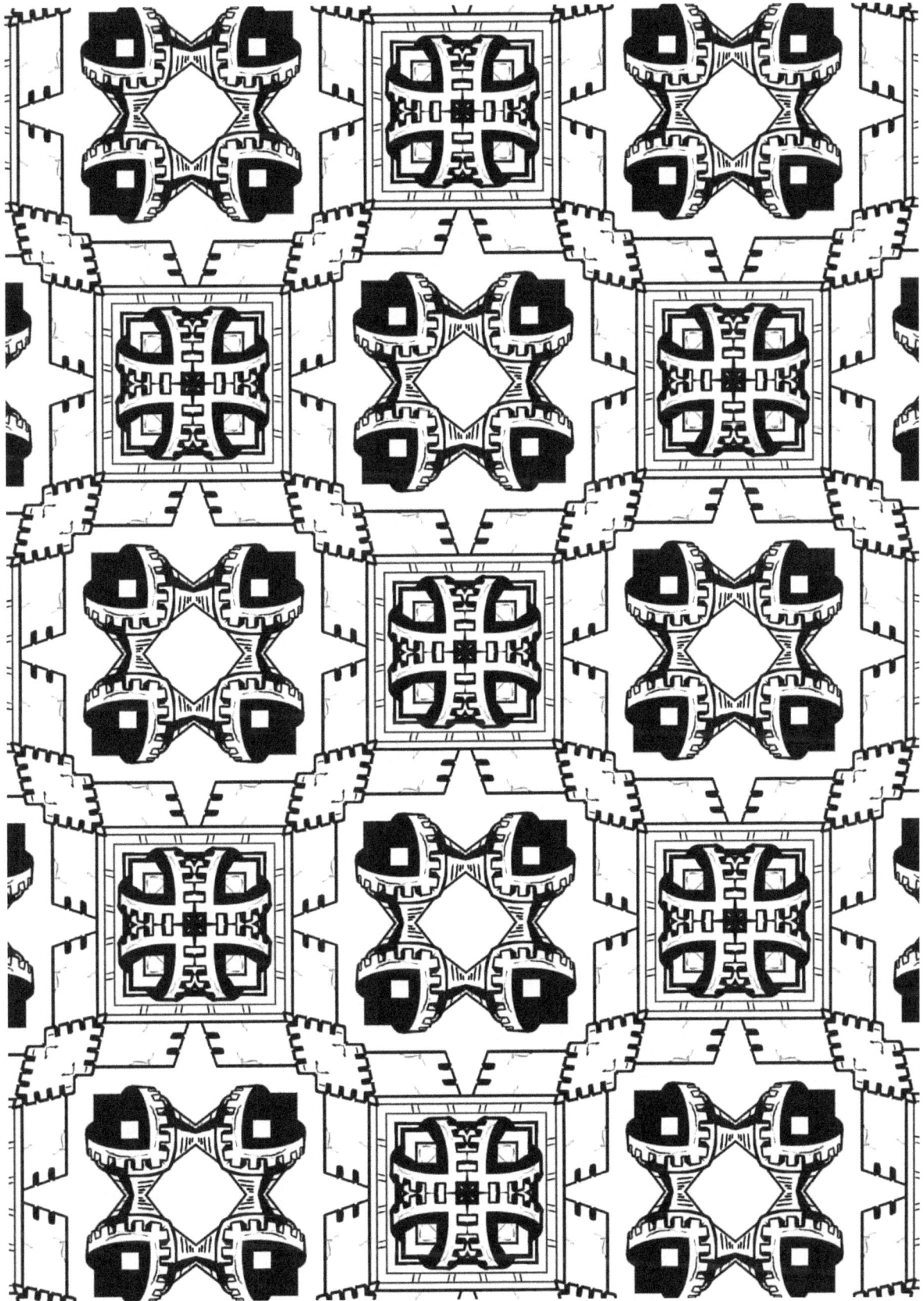

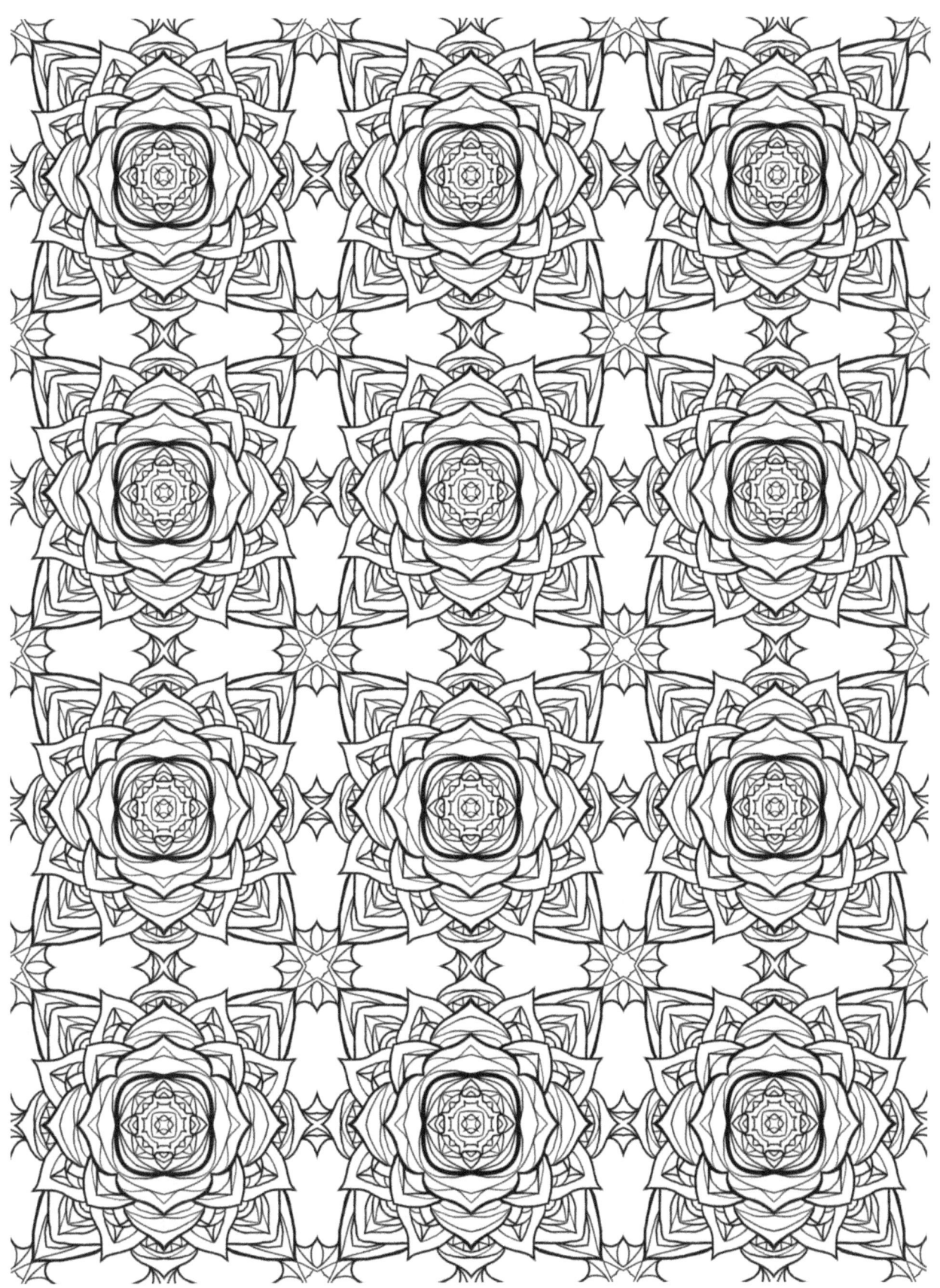

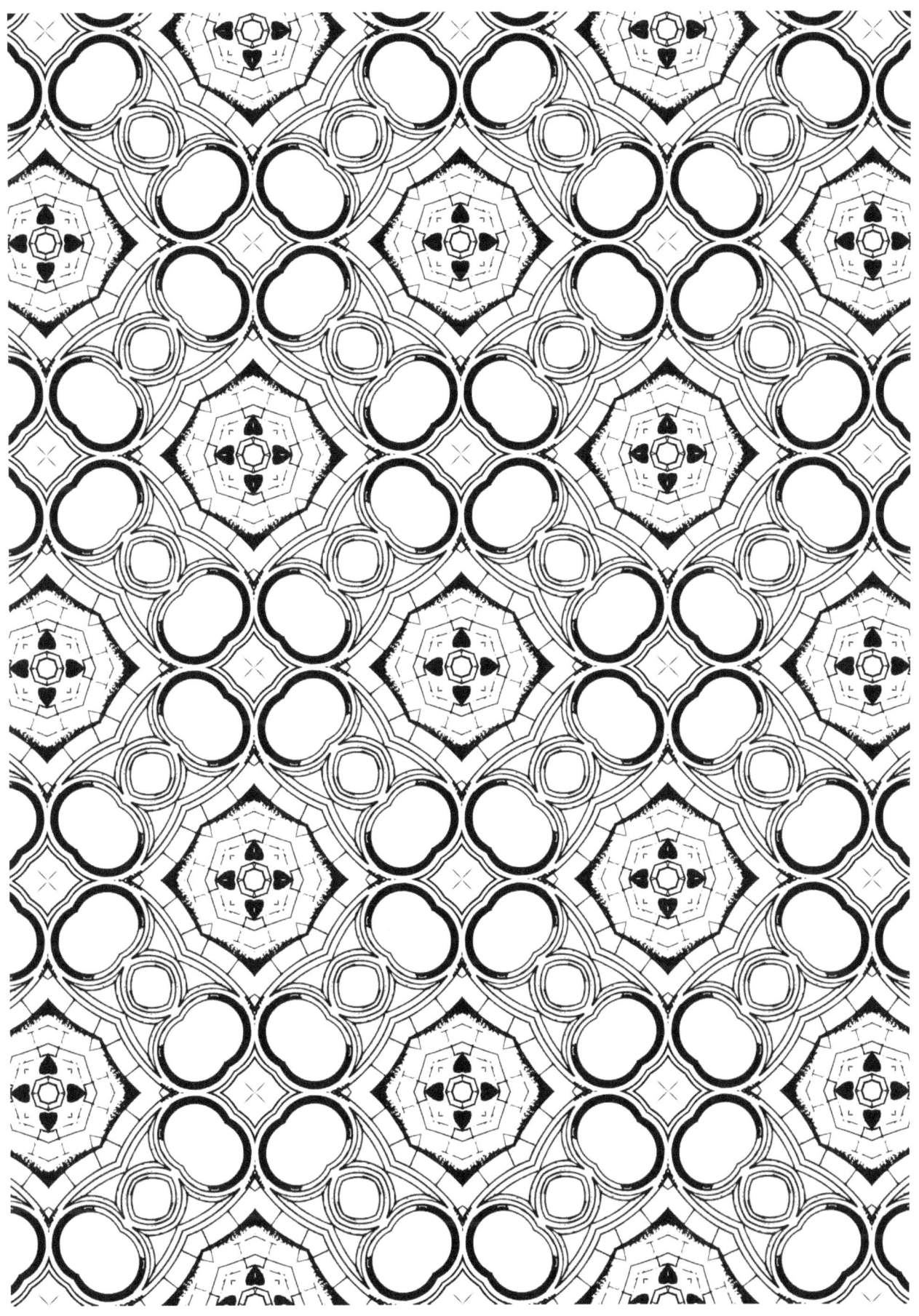

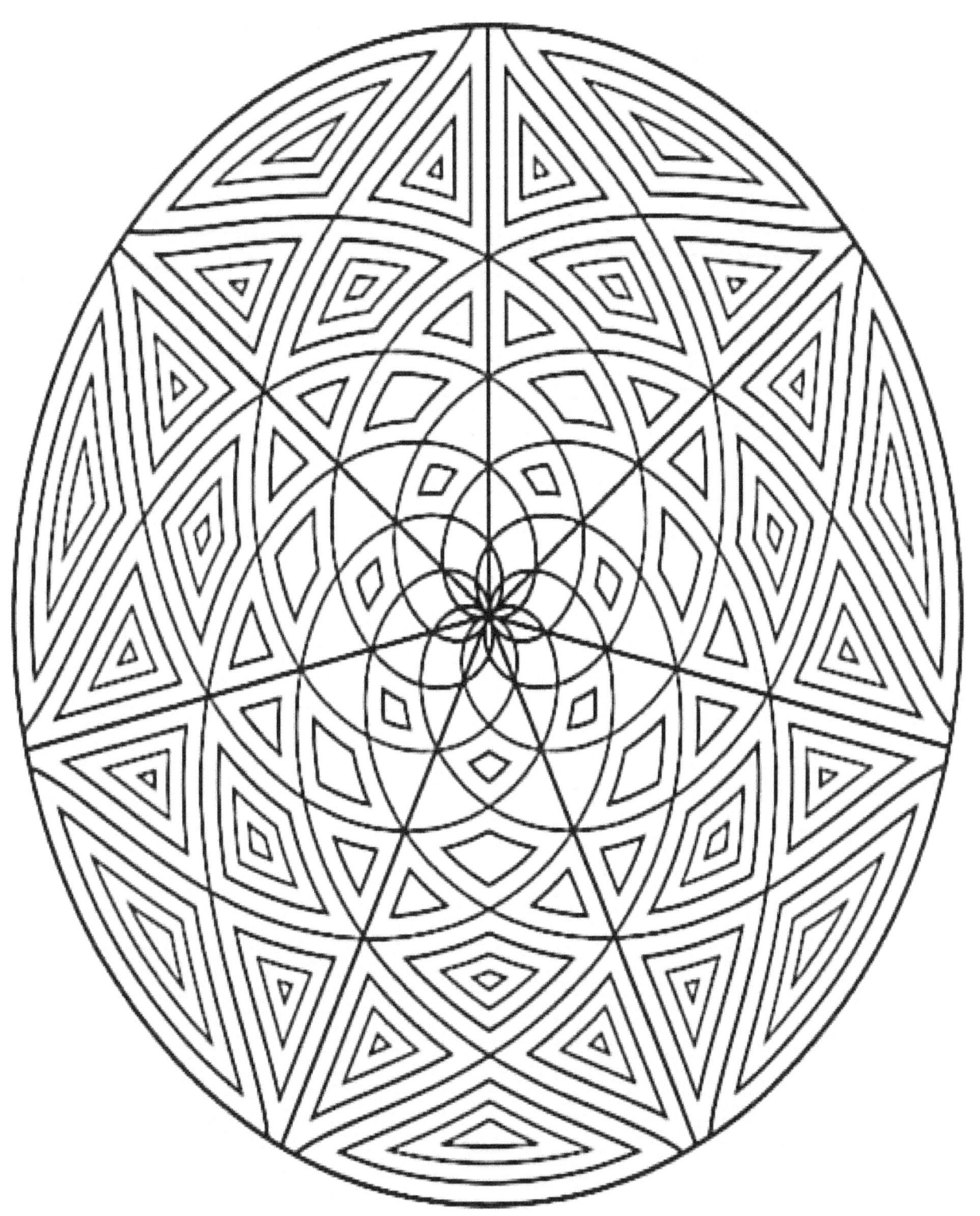

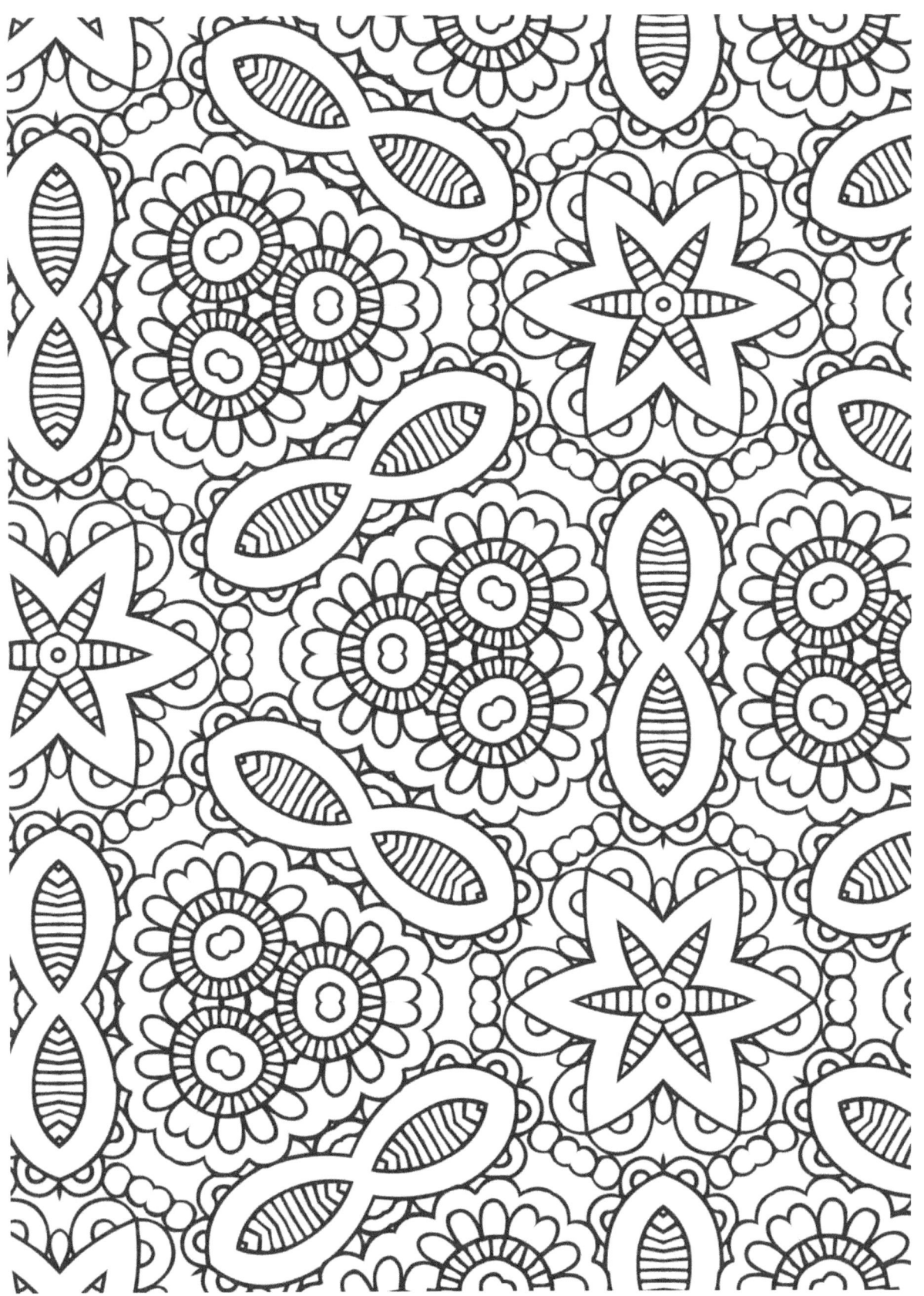

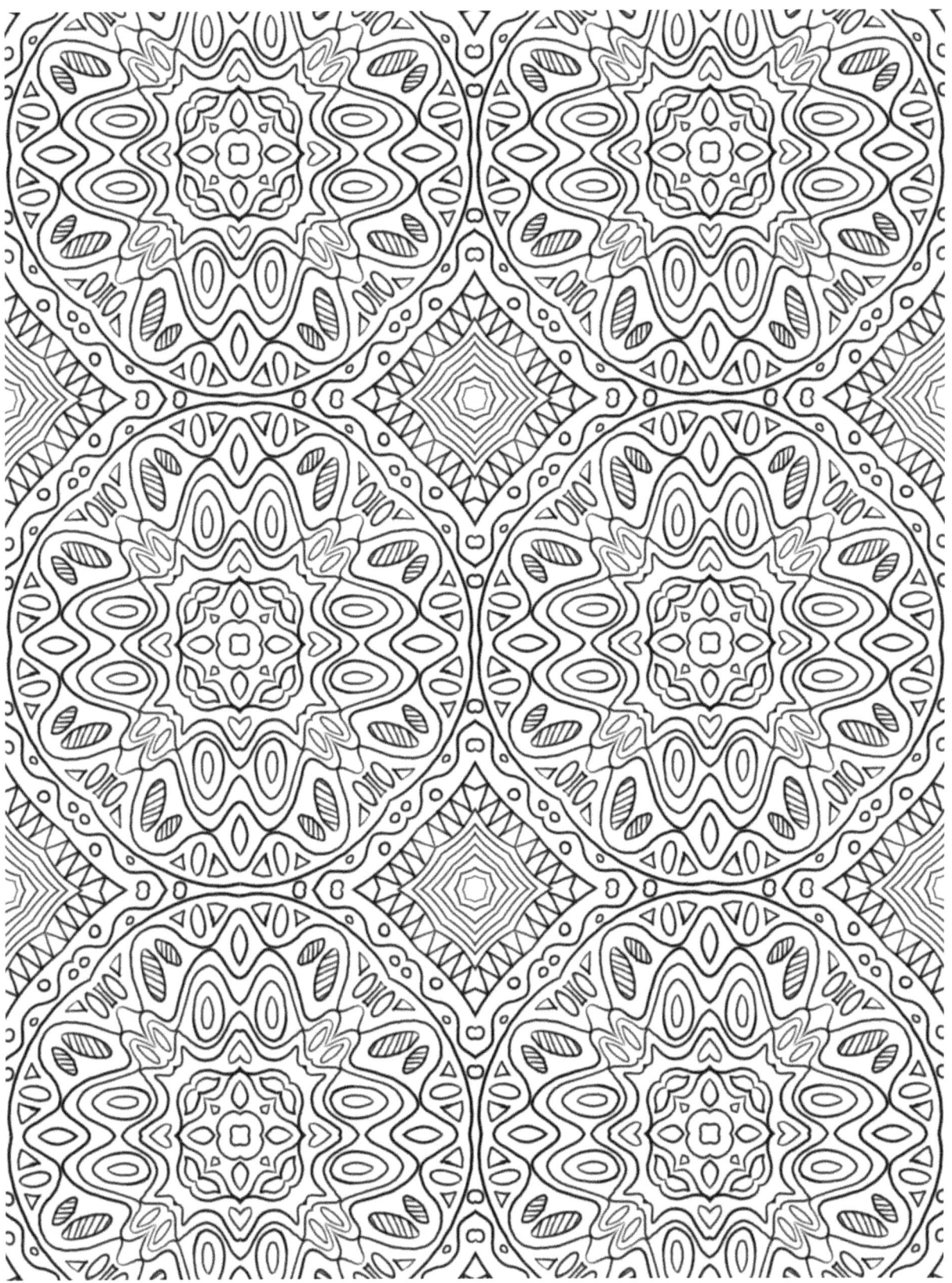

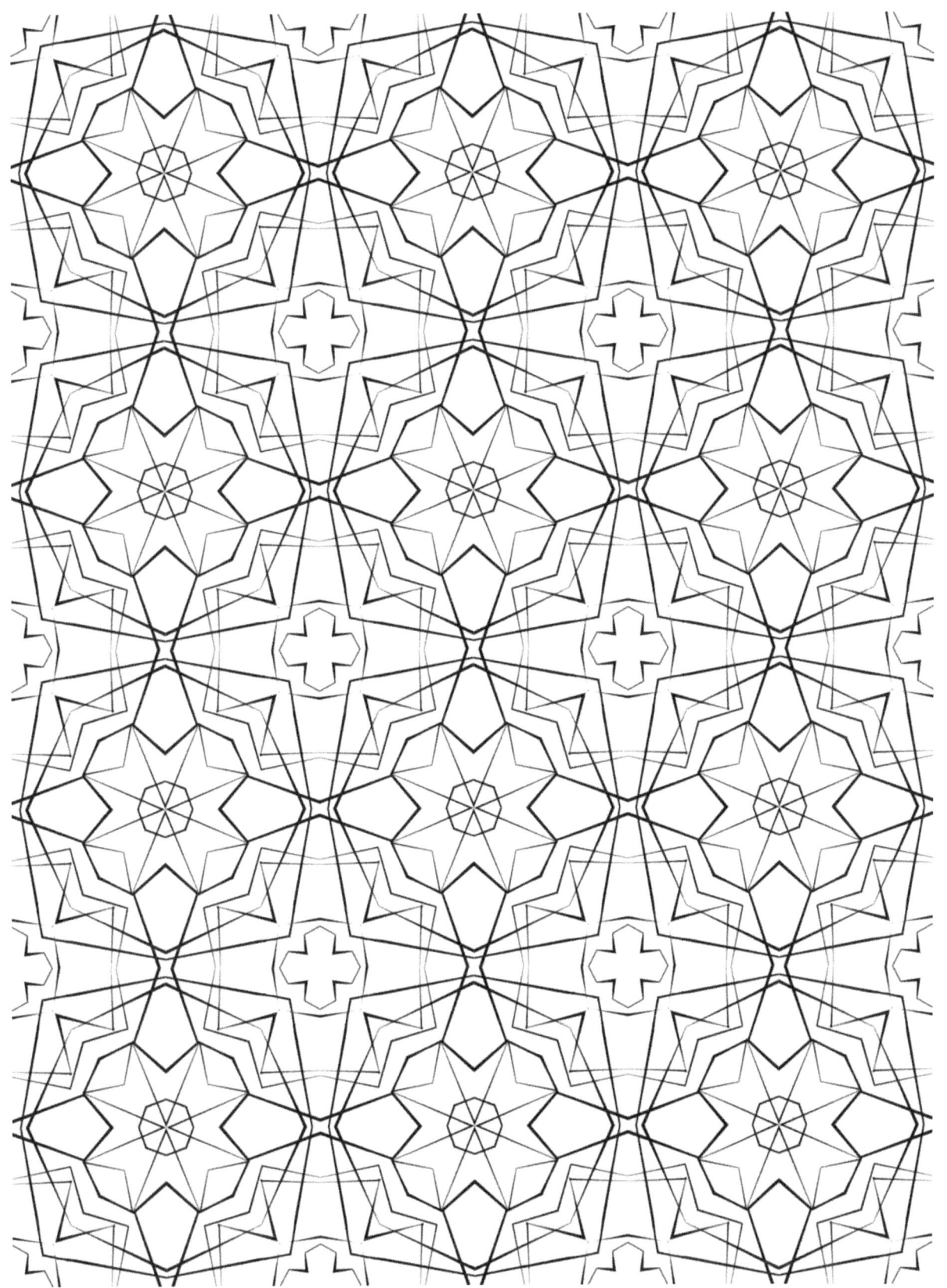

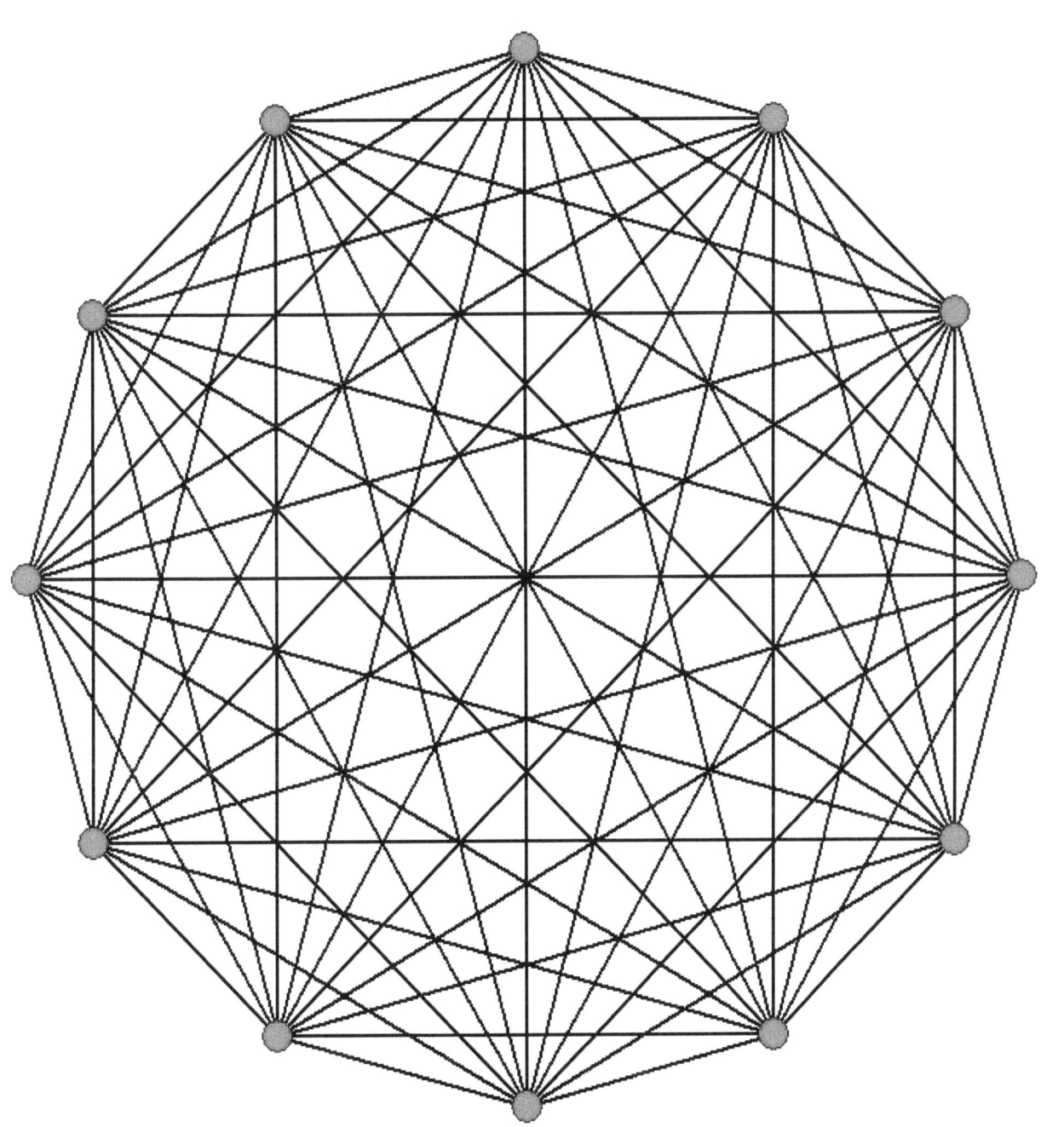

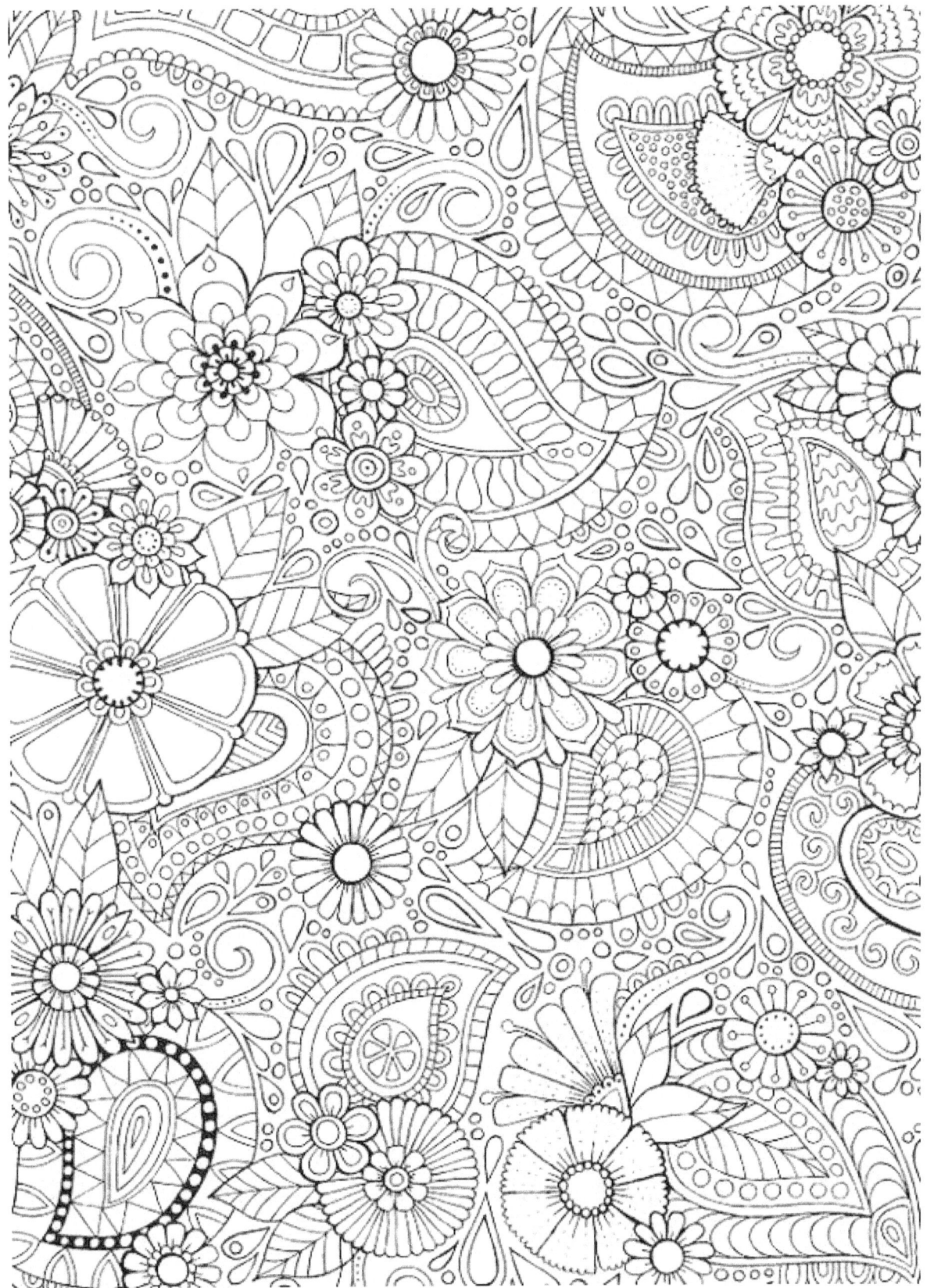

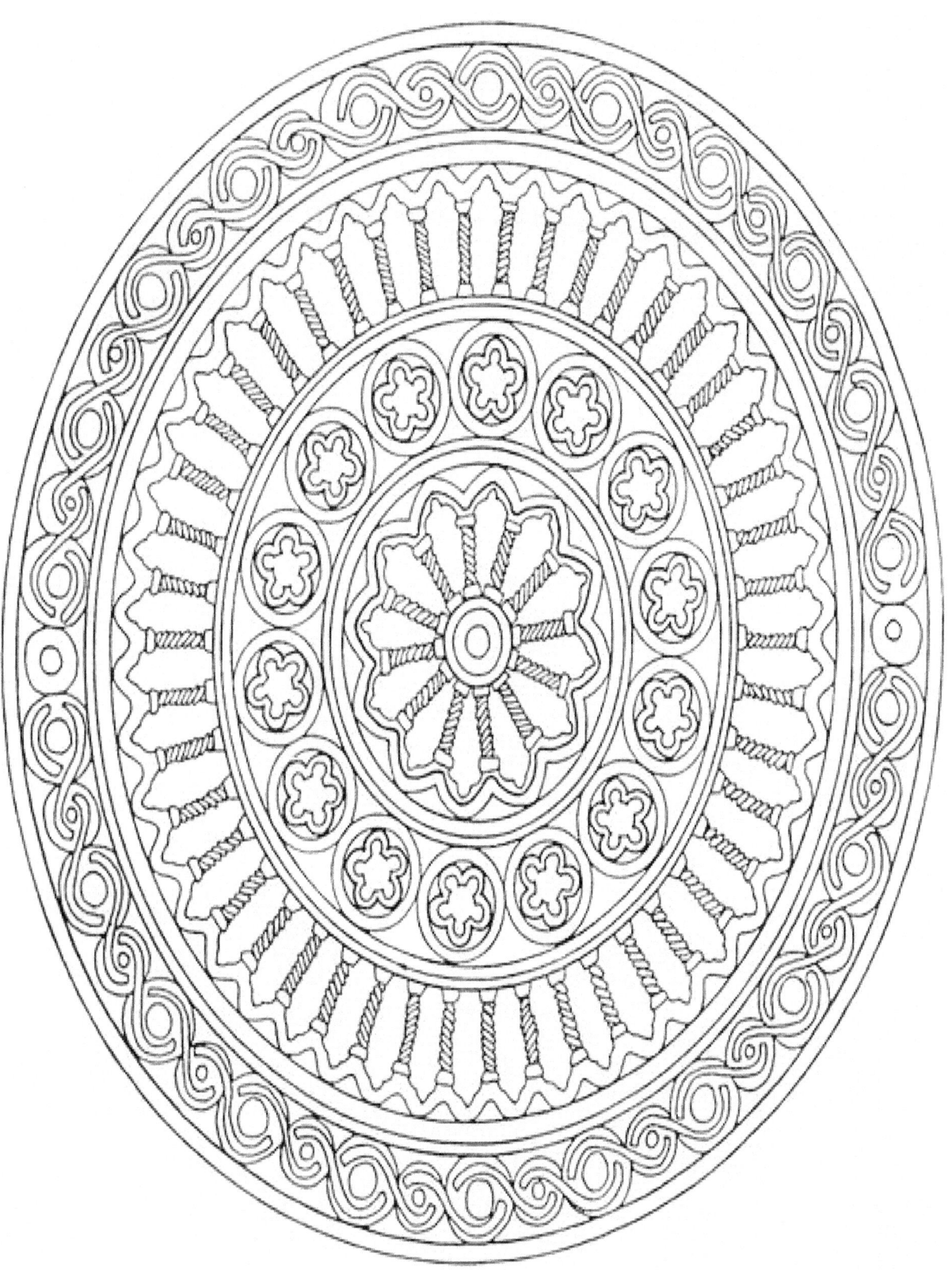

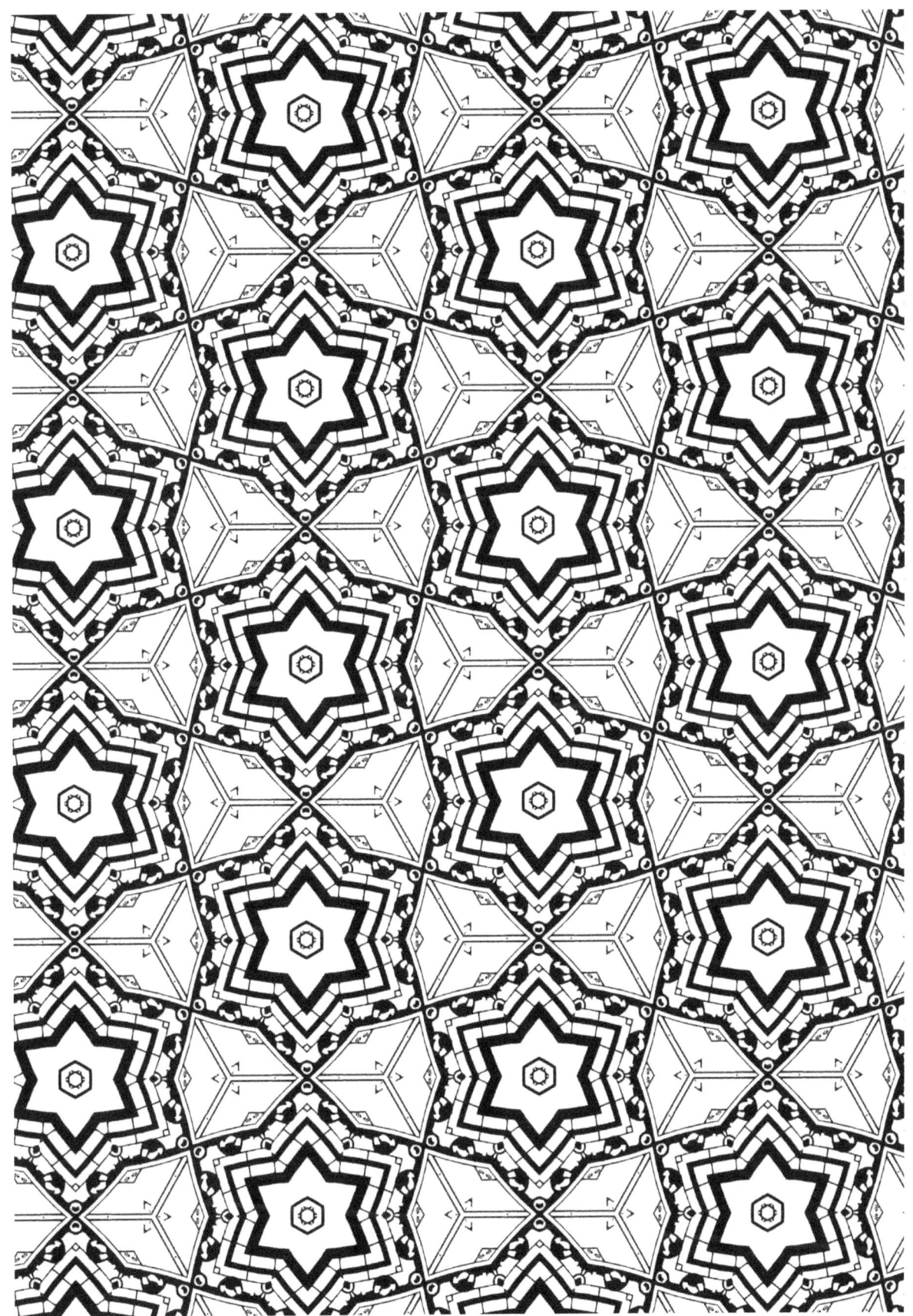

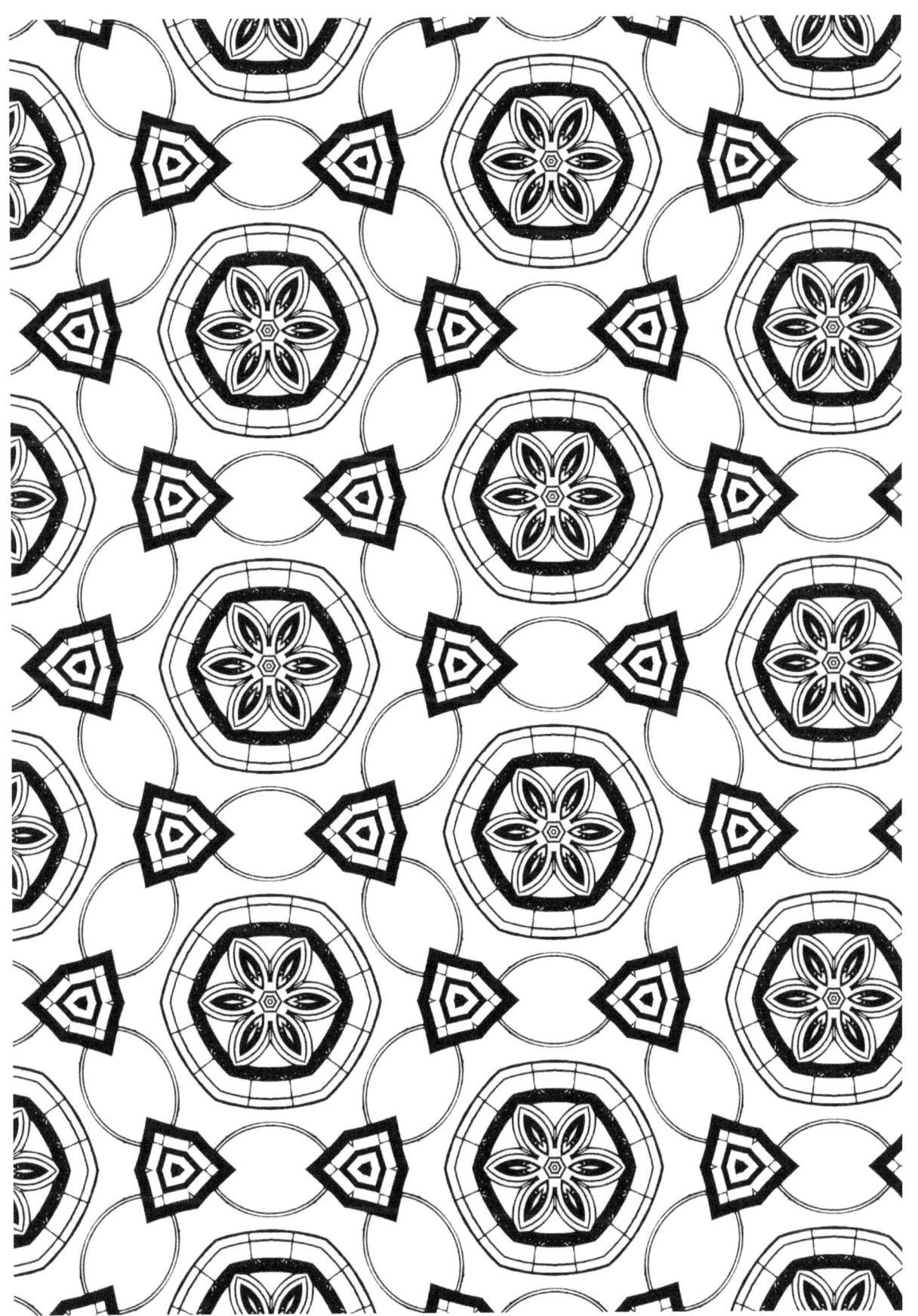

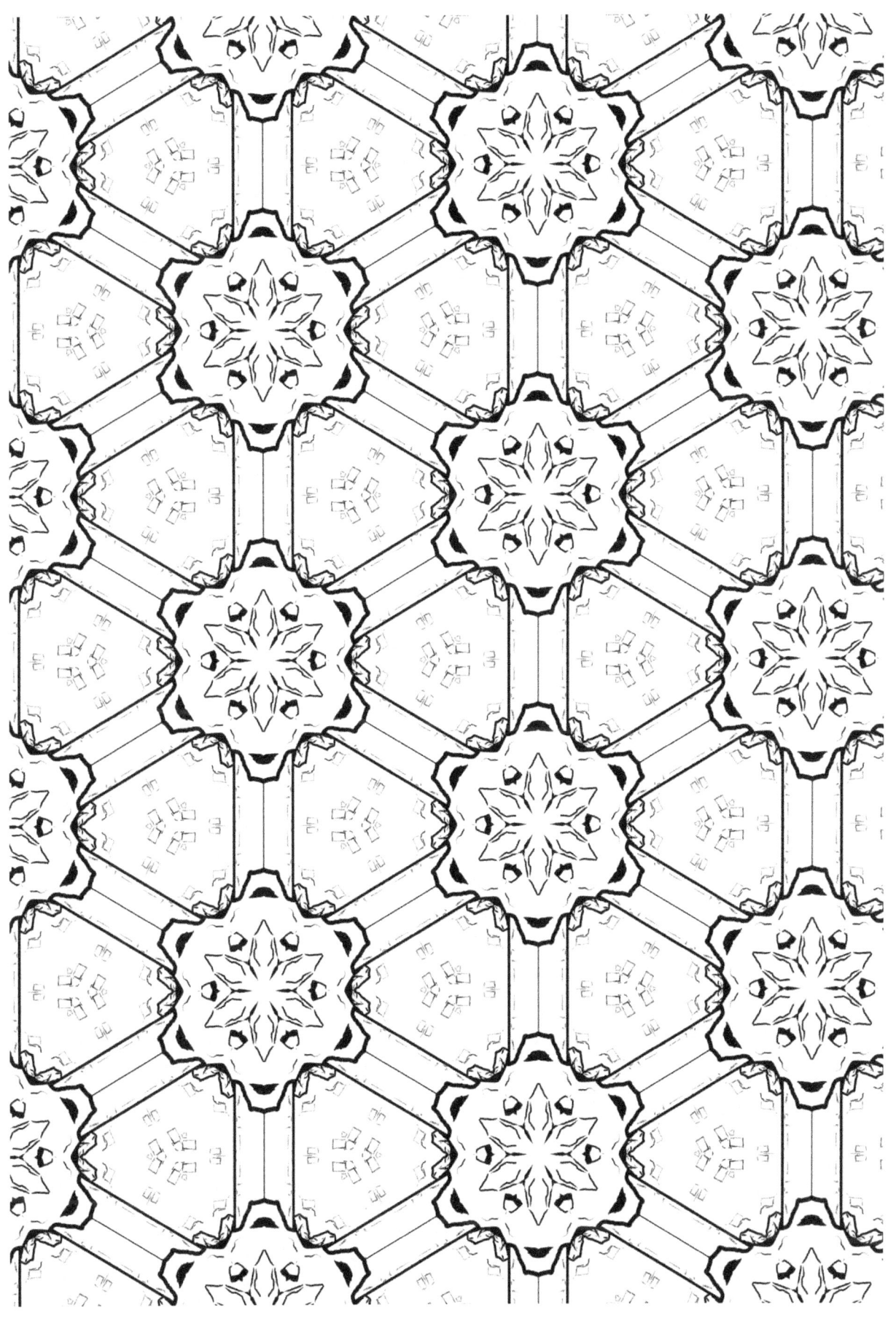

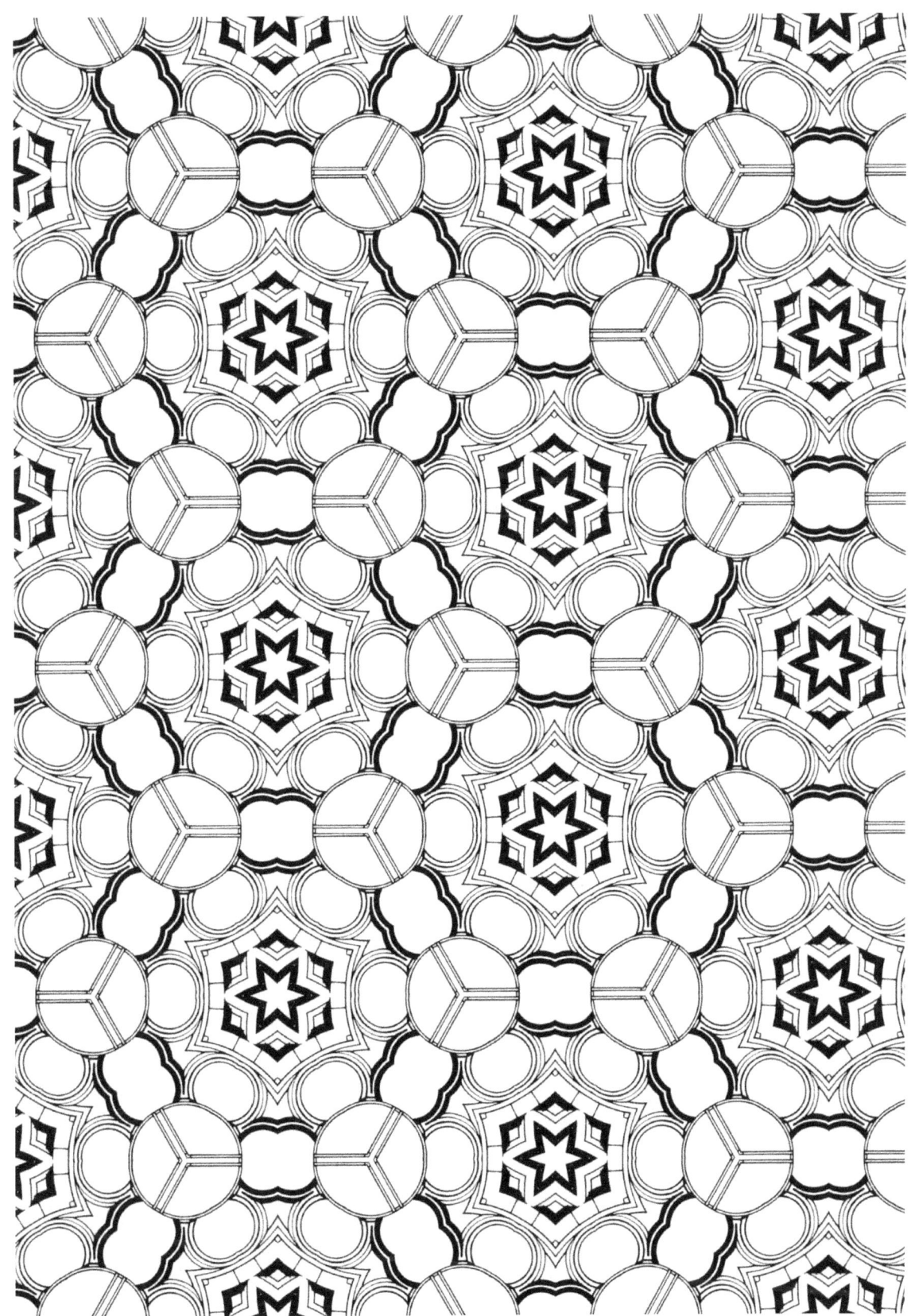

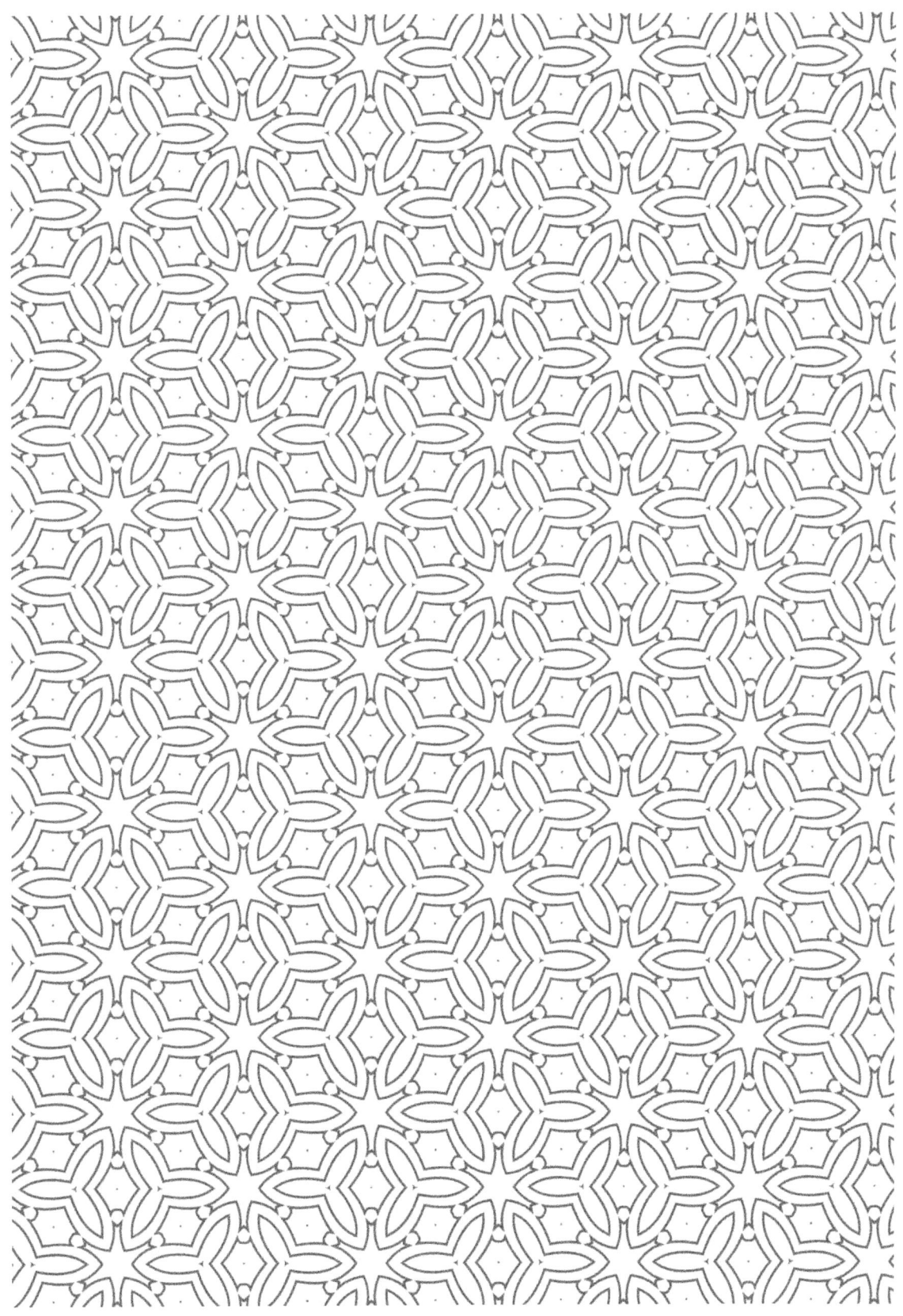

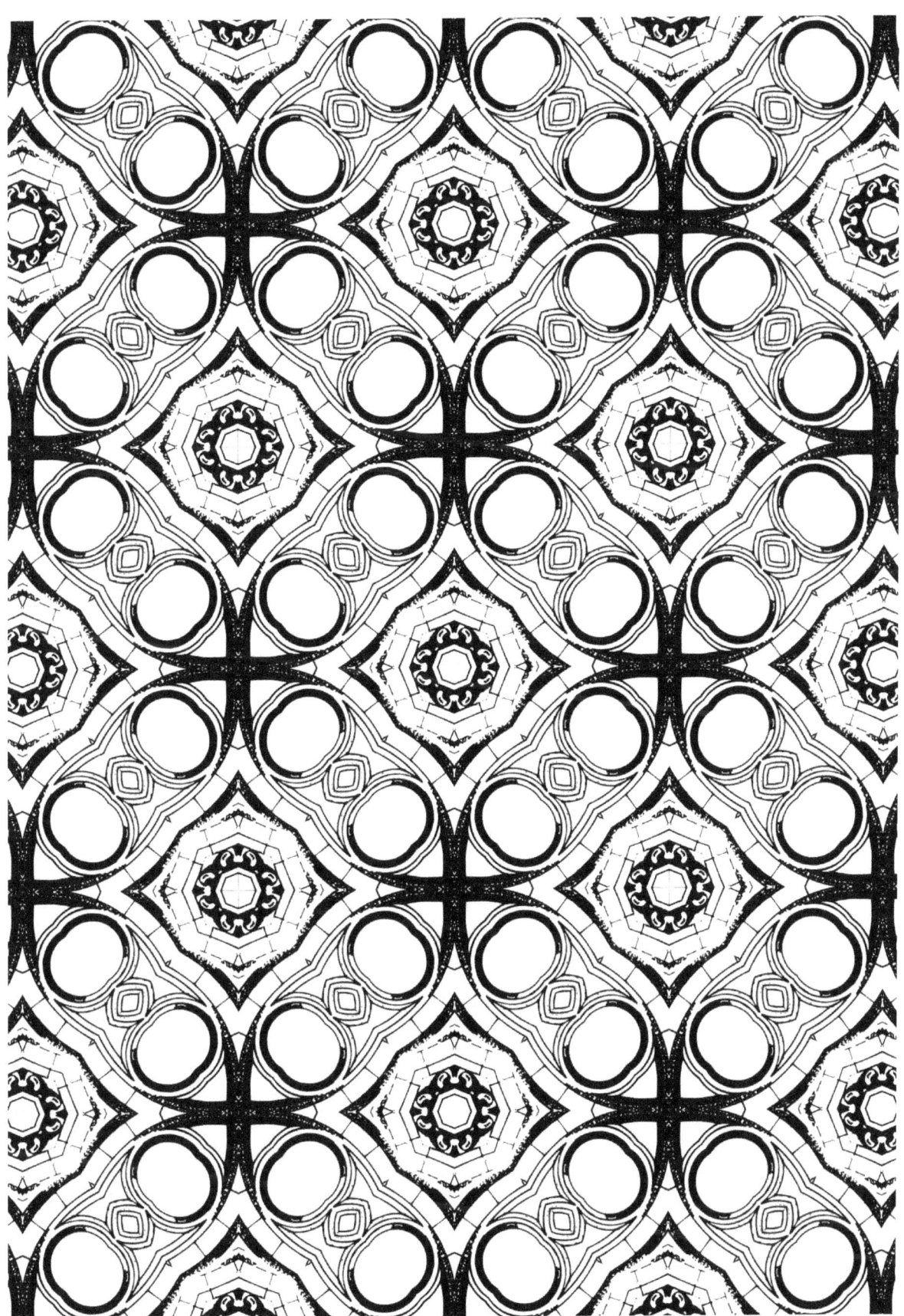

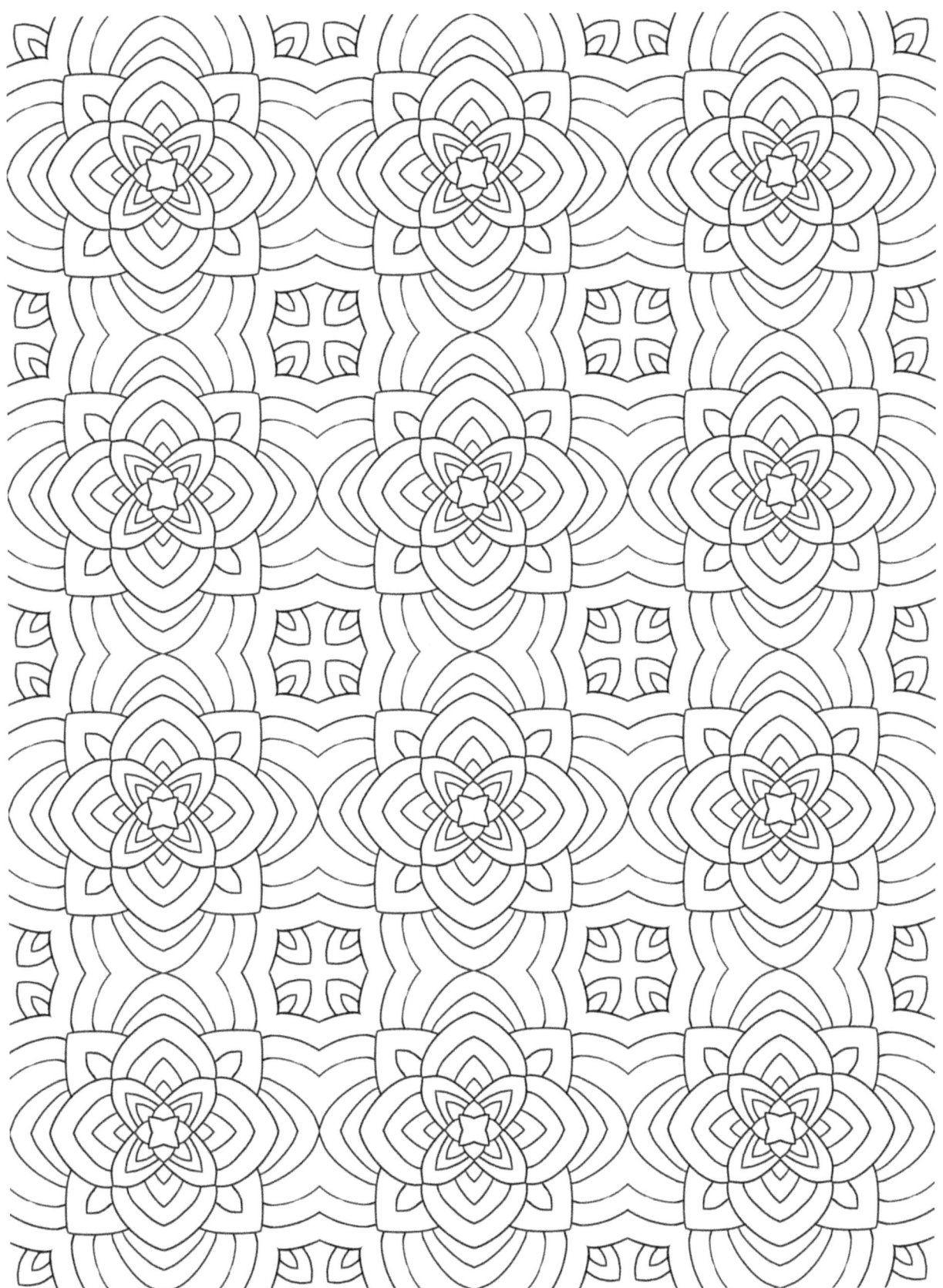

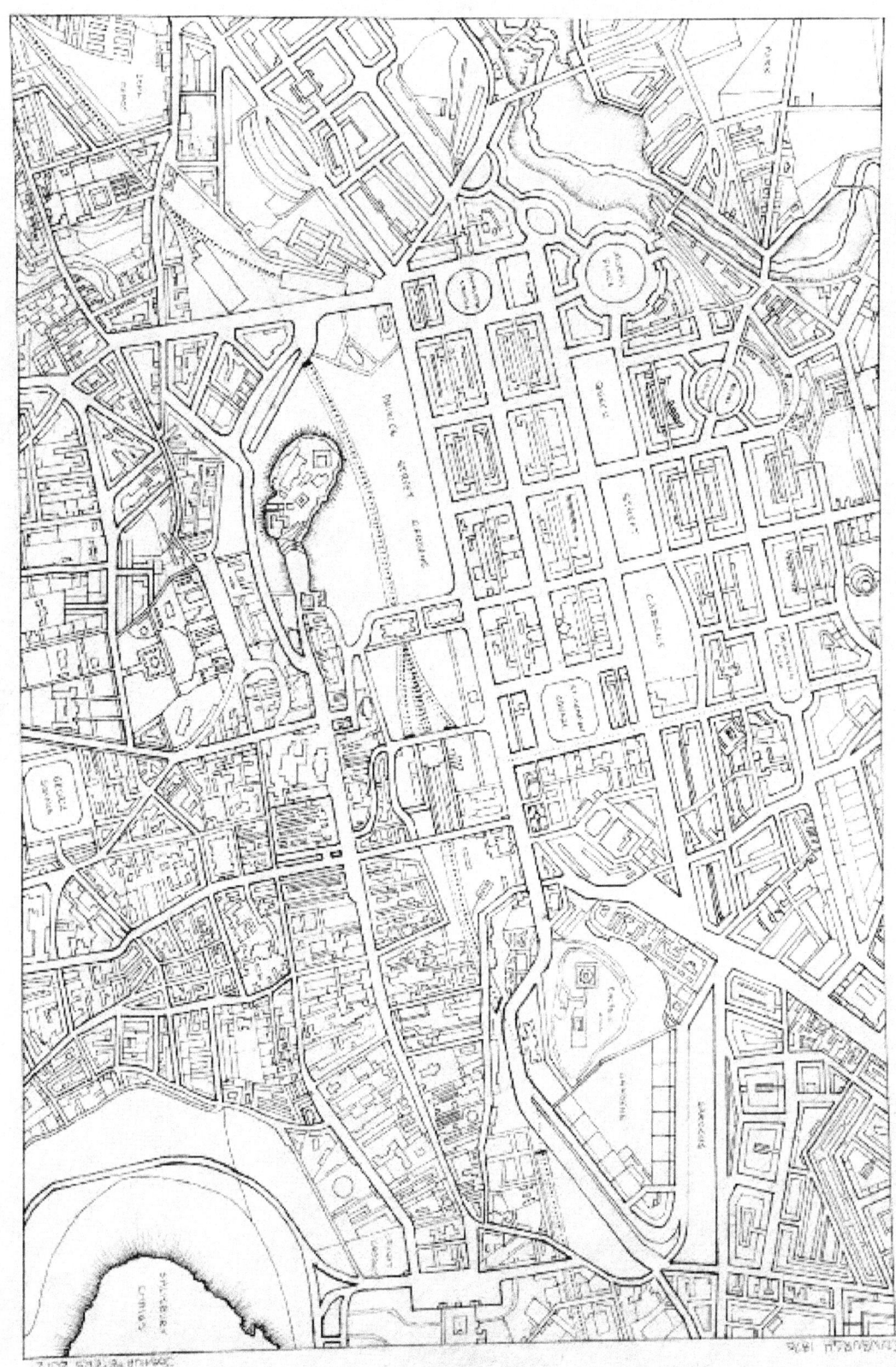

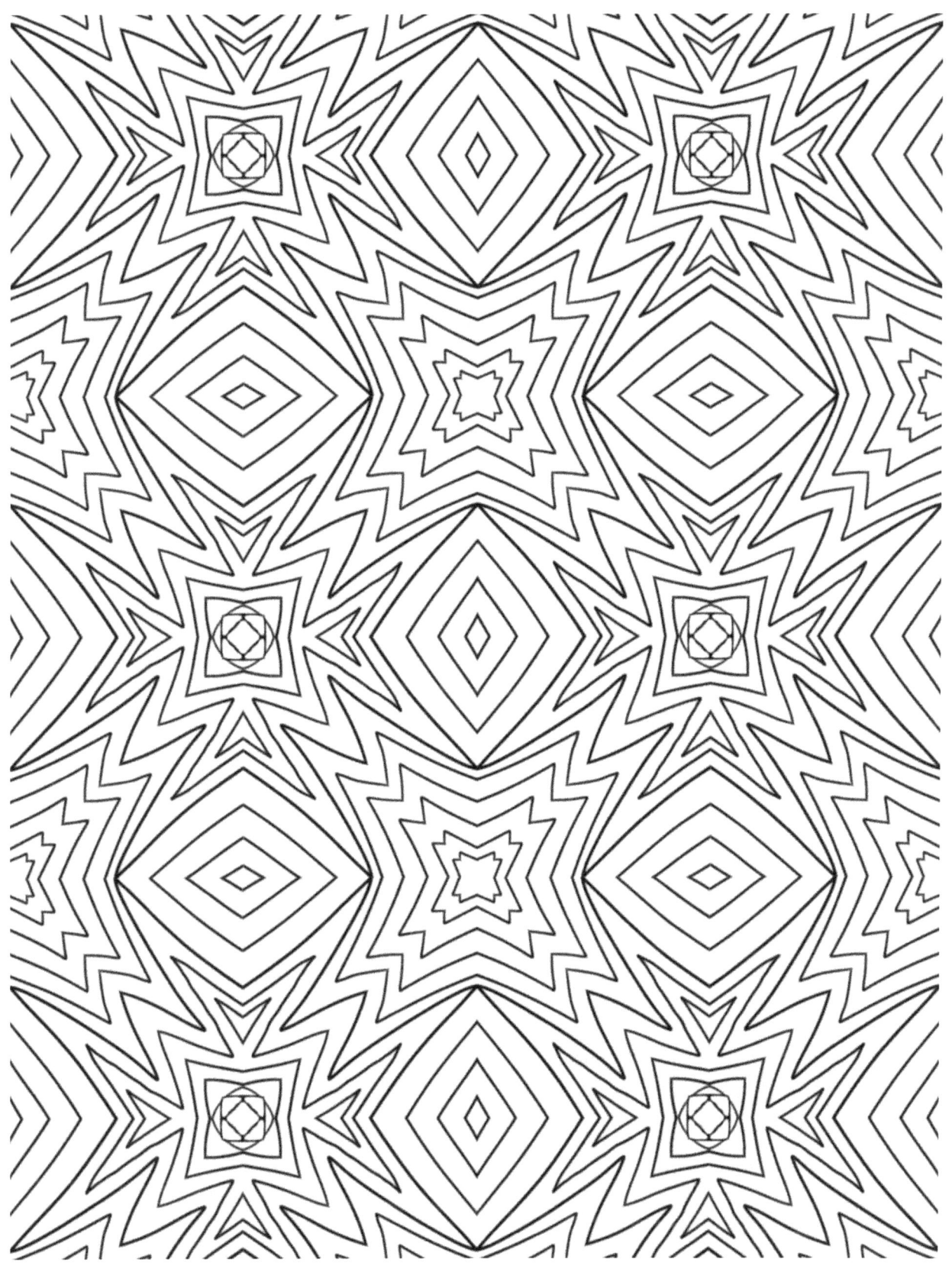

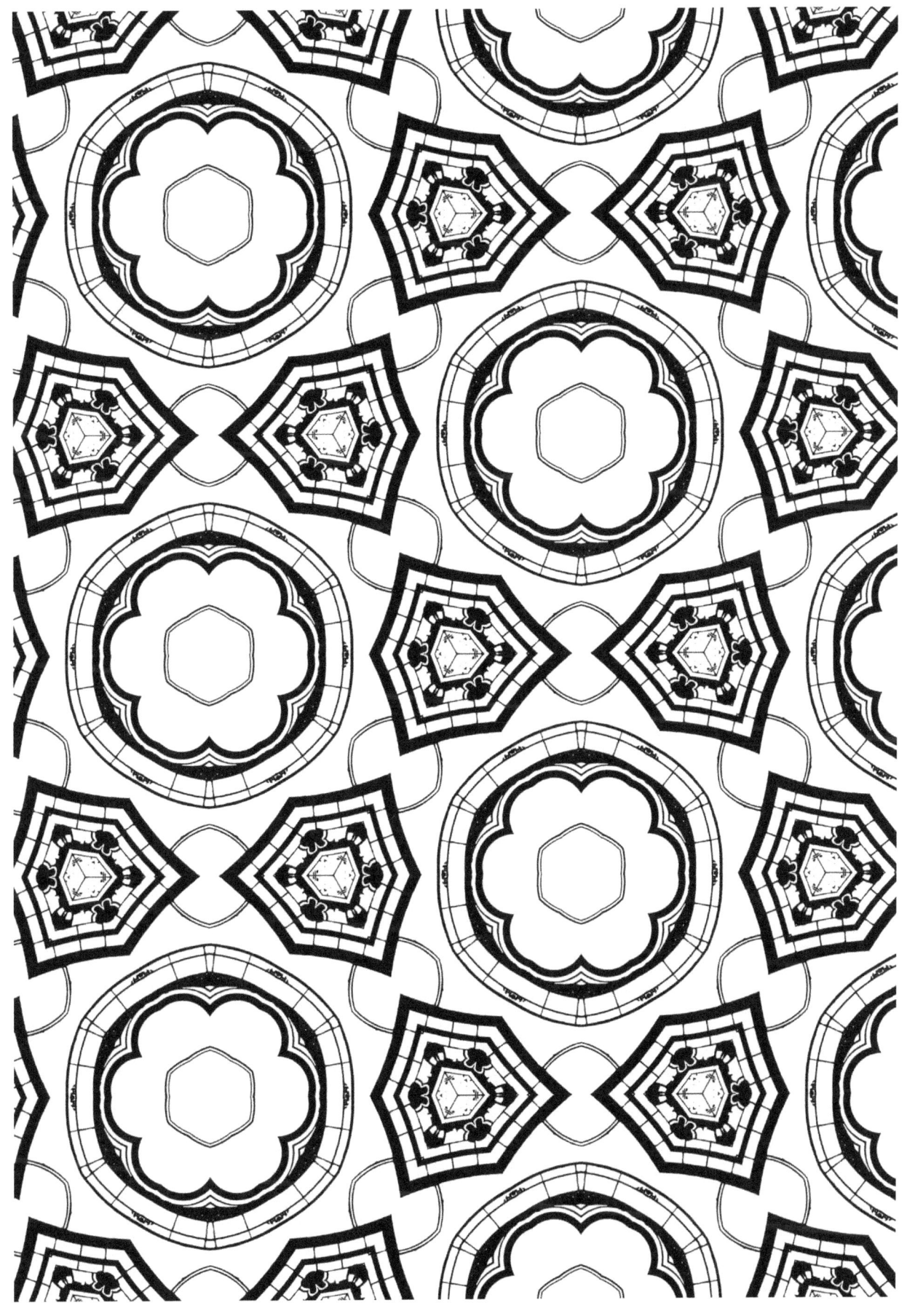

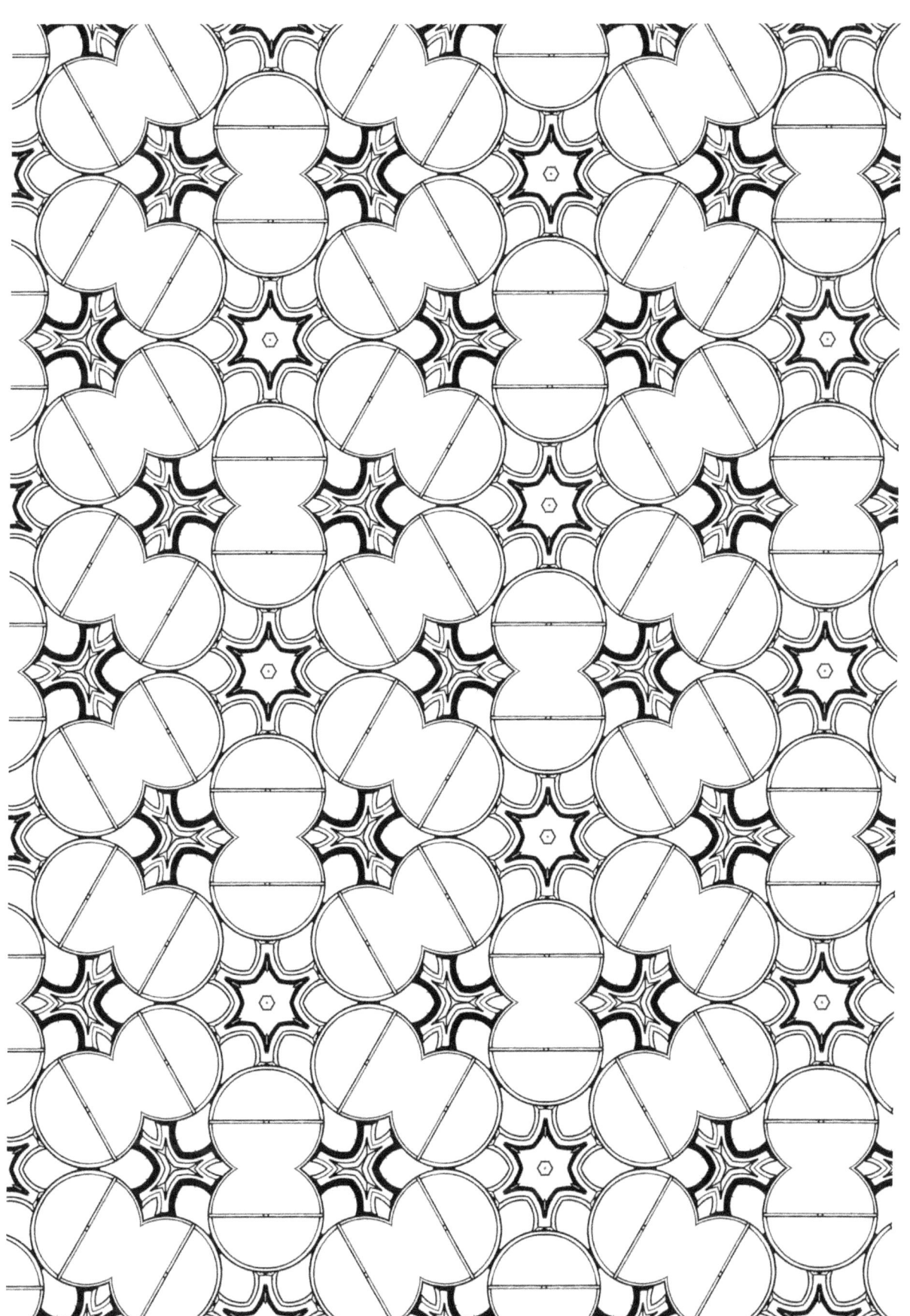

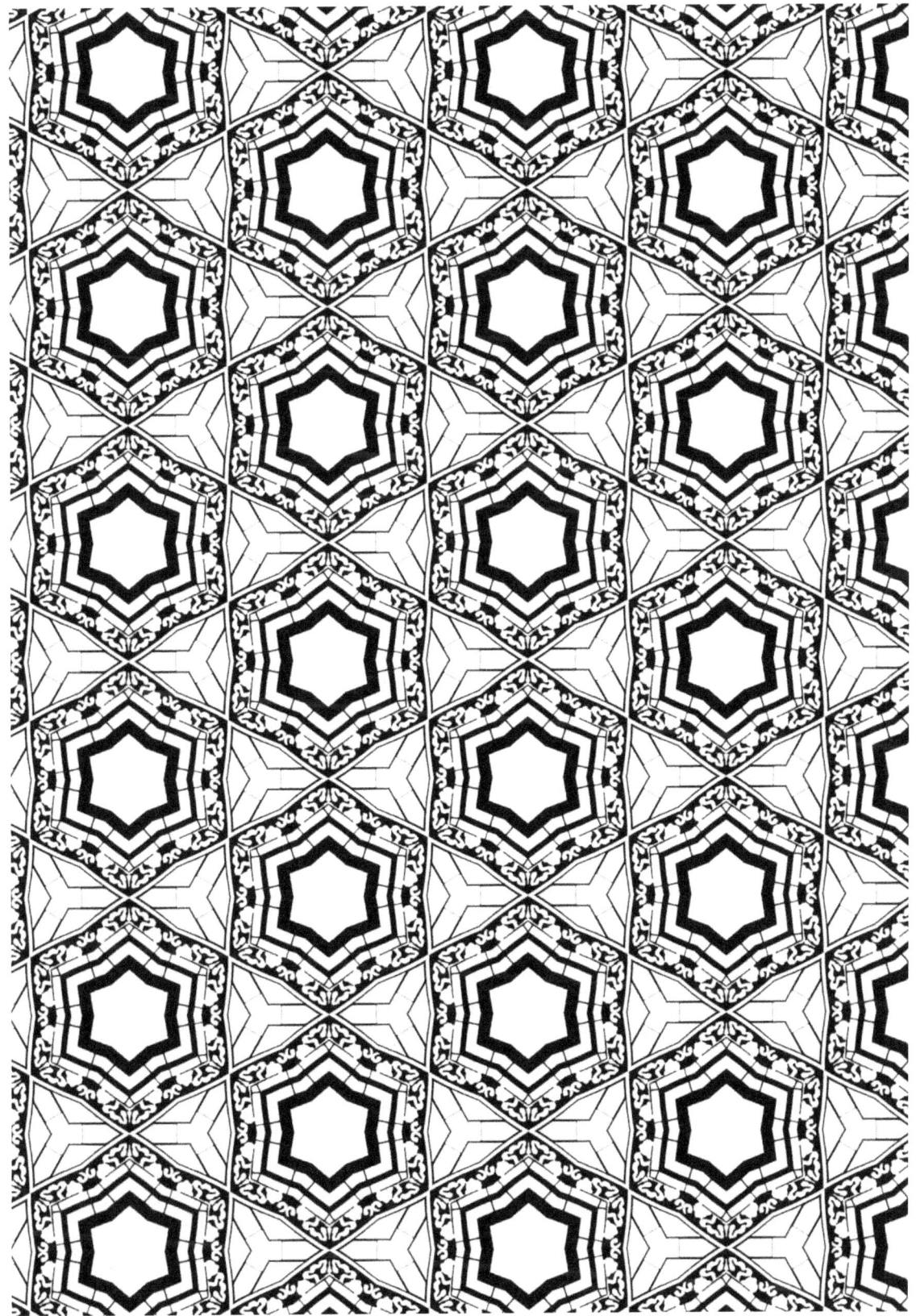

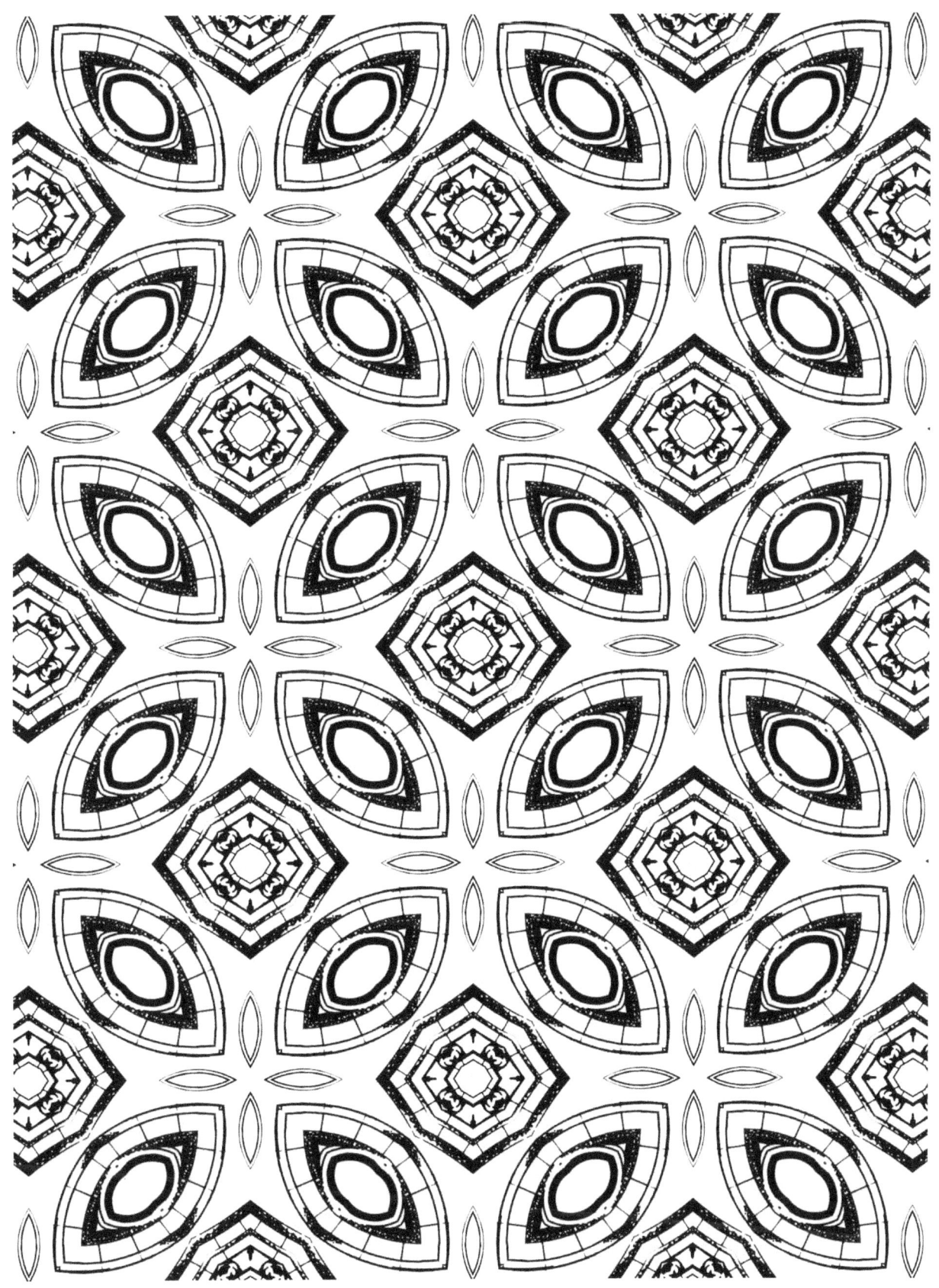

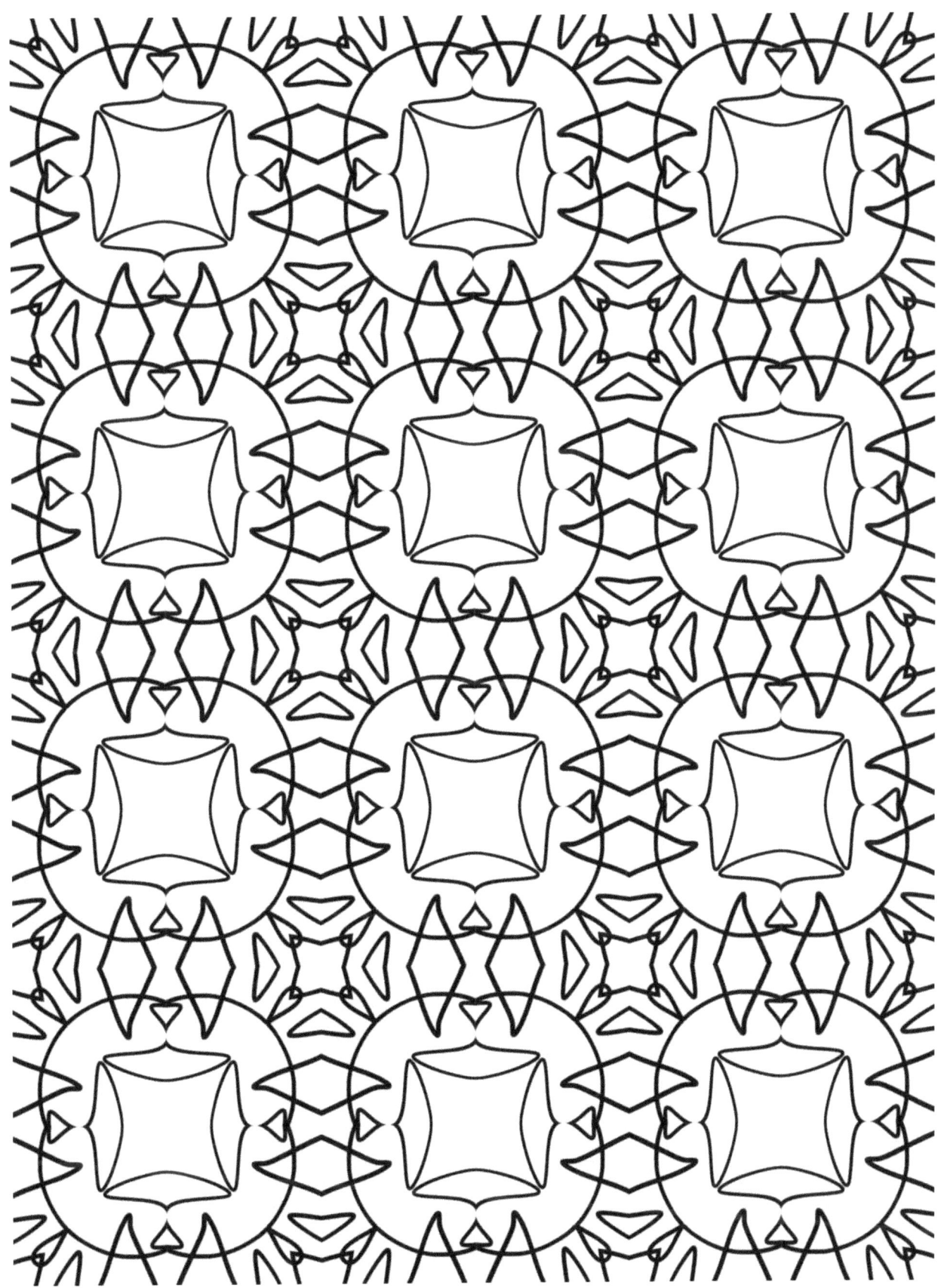

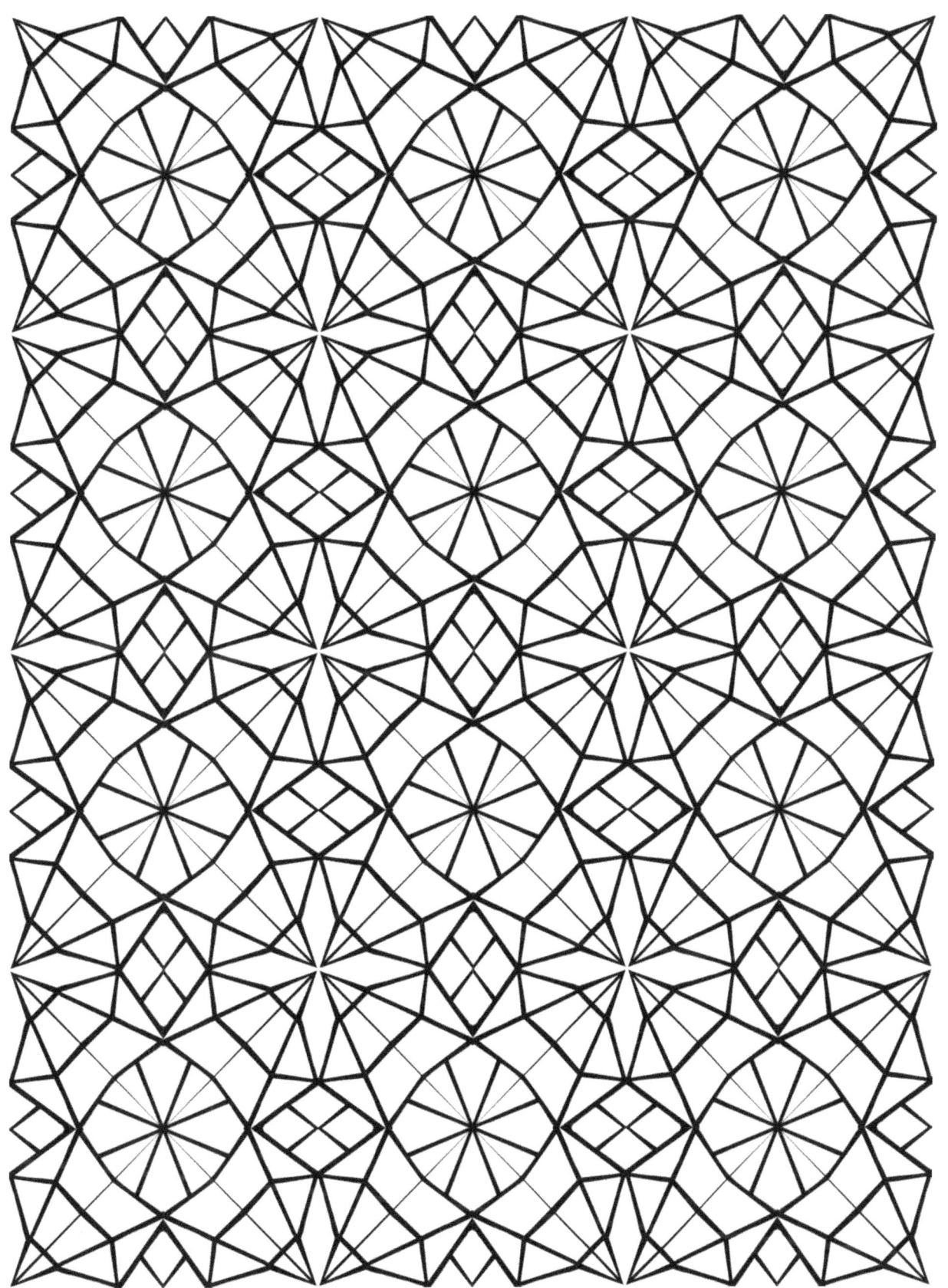

Introduction

 Though the first commercially successful adult coloring books were published in 2012 and 2013, the once-niche hobby has now grown into a full-on trend, with everyone from researchers at Johns Hopkins University to the editors of Yoga Journal suggesting coloring as an alternative to meditation. Here's why you might want to open a page and say ahhhhhh.

According to the American Art Therapy Association, art therapy is a mental health profession in which the process of making and creating artwork is used to "explore feelings, reconcile emotional conflicts, foster self-awareness, manage behavior and addictions, develop social skills, improve reality orientation, reduce anxiety and increase self-esteem." So basically, it's similar to good old therapy. Yet art therapy is not only about learning and improving yourself — it's a means of personal expression, too.

Just like meditation, coloring also allows us to switch off our brains from other thoughts and focus only on the moment, helping to alleviate free-floating anxiety. It can be particularly effective for people who aren't comfortable with more creatively expressive forms of art, says Marygrace Berberian, a certified art therapist and the Clinical Assistant Professor and Program Coordinator for the Graduate Art Therapy Program at NYU. "My experience has been that those participants who are more guarded find a lot of tranquility in coloring an image. It feels safer and it creates containment around their process," she adds.

For a more precise coloring experience we suggest using colored pencils or markers (thin tip) to make all of your pictures stand out.